FEARLESS

Scripture Edition

Contemplative Coloring for All People.

An exploration of original, hand drawn art by
Angel Cheney.

Art is a beautiful medium for relaxation, stress relief, therapy, and enjoyment. It is our hope that as you travel through these pages you will be encouraged by what you find and experience. Some of the pages include areas of white space where you can add your own thoughts, dreams, or doodles. Enjoy!

About the artist:
Angel Cheney is an artist, singer/songwriter, poet, and author from the Indianapolis, IN area. She is passionate about taking people on a journey with her through art, words, and music. Check out more of her work at:

www.angelcheney.com

Stay tuned!
Exciting new books of
Contemplative Coloring
for All People
COMING SOON!

THE LORD IS MY LIGHT AND MY SALVATION; WHOM SHALL
I FEAR? THE LORD IS THE STRONGHOLD OF MY LIFE; OF
WHOM SHALL I BE AFRAID?

PSALM 27:1

Speak the TRUTH
you are carrying in your heart
like hidden treasure.

Jesus,
guard my
heart
with your
peace.

TRUTH

Peace I leave with you; my
peace I give to you. I do not
give as the world gives. Do not
let your [heart] be troubled,
and do not let it be afraid.   John 14:27

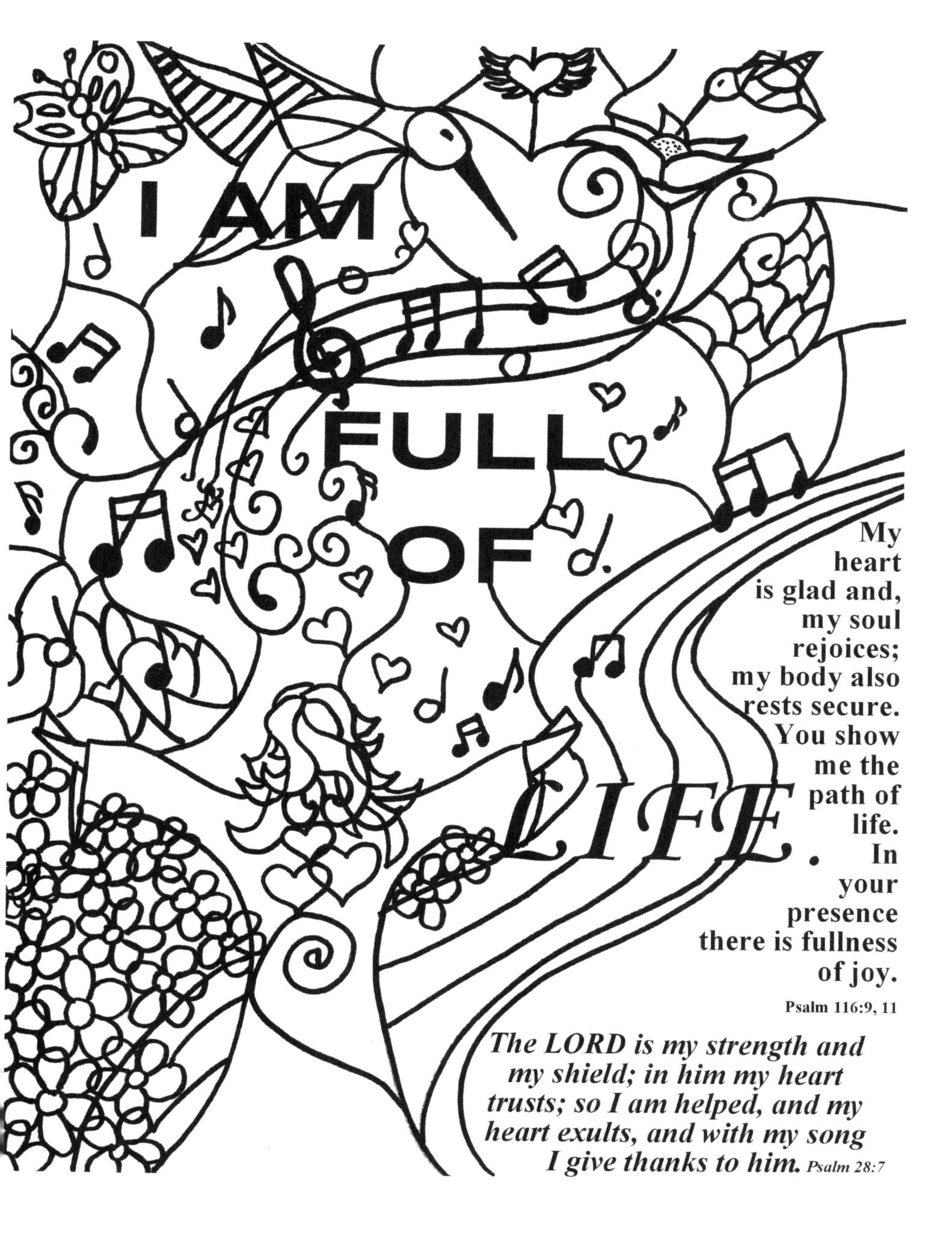

I AM FULL OF LIFE

My heart is glad and, my soul rejoices; my body also rests secure. You show me the path of life. In your presence there is fullness of joy. Psalm 116:9, 11

The LORD is my strength and my shield; in him my heart trusts; so I am helped, and my heart exults, and with my song I give thanks to him. Psalm 28:7

I AM

OVERFLOWING

WITH

LOVE

Even though I walk through the darkest valley, I will fear no evil; for you are with me...

You anoint my head with oil; my cup overflows. Surely goodness and mercy shall follow me all the days of my life, and I shall dwell in the house of the LORD my whole life long.

Psalm 23: 4-6

I am peacefully allowing my life to unfold.

**Those of steadfast mind [God keeps] in peace-
in peace because they trust in [him]. Isaiah 26:3**

STRENGTH

I
CAN
DO
ALL
THINGS

THROUGH
HIM

WHO
GIVES
ME

STRENGTH.

PHILIPPIANS 4:13

I

AM

SAFE

Whoever dwells in the shelter
of the Most High
will rest in the shadow of the Almighty.
He will cover you with his feathers,
and under his wings you will find refuge.

Psalm 91:1, 4

My child,
if you accept my words
and treasure up
my commandments
within you...
wisdom will come
into your heart,
and knowledge will be
pleasant to your soul...
understanding
will guard you.

Proverbs 2:1, 10-11

Breathe in peace
LET IT
Breathe out...
Breathe in peace...

I AM
LETTING GO
OF THE PAST,
PRESENT
IN THIS MOMENT,

AND MOVING
FORWARD
WITH
CONFIDENCE.

Blessed is the one who trusts in the LORD, whose confidence is in him.

Jeremiah 17:7

In all
things
we are more
than
CONQUERORS
through him
who loved
us.

[Nothing]
will be able
to separate
us from the
love of God
in Christ
Jesus our
Lord.
Romans 8:37, 39

LOVE
ENABLES
ME
TO BE
A
CONQUEROR.

I AM GRATEFUL FOR:

1.

2.

3.

4.

5.

IT IS GOOD TO GIVE THANKS TO THE LORD.

PSALM 92:1

I am beautiful

I am loved

I AM ENOUGH

And Jesus stopped and said,
"Call him here." So they called
the blind man, saying to him,
"Take courage, stand up!
He is calling for you."

Mark 10:49

COURAGE

EMBRACE
LOVE,

RELEASE
FEAR.

I AM

ANCHORED

IN PEACE.

And the peace of God, which surpasses all understanding, will
guard your [heart] and [mind] in Christ Jesus.
Philippians 4:7

Those who wait for the LORD
shall renew their strength,
they shall mount up
with wings like eagles.

Isaiah 40:31

Plant truth
and reap
a harvest
of
LOVE.

For God has not given us
a spirit of fear, but a spirit of
POWER, and of LOVE,
and of a SOUND MIND.

2 Timothy 1:7

Finally, be strong in the LORD
and in his mighty power.
Put on the full armor of God,
so that you can take your
stand.

Ephesians 6:10-11

I

AM

BRAVE.

Design your own coat of arms

I LOVE AND DEEPLY CARE FOR MY MIND, BODY, AND SOUL.

It was you who formed my inward parts; you knit me together in my mother's womb. I praise you because I am fearfully and wonderfully made... My frame was not hidden from you, when I was being made in secret, intricately woven in the depths of the earth.

Psalm 139:13-15

God
[will give you]
the mantle of praise
instead of a faint spirit.

[You] will be called
[an oak] of righteousness,
the planting of the LORD
to display his glory.

Isaiah 61:3

www.ingramcontent.com/pod-product-compliance
Lightning Source LLC
Chambersburg PA
CBHW081153040426

42445CB00015B/1865